abc OF
MOTO

C000059751

by

JOHN
DUDLEY

LONDON :

Ian Allan Ltd

INTRODUCTION

L ONG before the average schoolboy thinks in terms of buying a motor car, he is examining motor cycle catalogues with a discriminating eye, and doing his best to identify the makes of machine on the road. Here he is faced with a difficult task for, while the motor car manufacturers provide distinctive radiator grilles and have long established external characteristics by which their products can be identified, the motor cycle is composed almost entirely of frame, petrol tank, engine and wheels.

In the following pages I have attempted to offer some recognition features which will assist the spotter, and to indicate the chief points of interest to the prospective buyer. The petrol tank is a good place to start when identifying a machine, for inevitably it carries the maker's name or trademark. A particular model is usually finished in a specific colour when it leaves the factory, and these colours are mentioned in the descriptions, although it should be remembered that they sometimes alter from year to year, and a machine may have been repainted or produced in a special colour scheme. In some cases, too, the engine type is a useful recognition point—the Vincent vee twin and the sloping Panther 100 are good examples.

The great motor cycle industry of this country presents a most varied selection of machines—from the two stroke 98 c.c. James and Commander models, capable of from 40 to 50 m.p.h., to the new 100 m.p.h. Royal Enfield Meteor 700, the largest of British twins, and the four cylinder Square Four Ariel. In the field of luxury high performance models British supremacy is well established, and more lightweights are available than ever before. The demand for economical motoring has led to developments in the field of autocycles and three-wheelers as well ; thus a special section has been devoted to them.

Space permits description of a cross section only of the industry's products, and it is regretted that some makes have had to be omitted. In the motor cycle racing sphere British machines are supreme, and while some action shots of famous models are included, the racing motor cycles are not described in detail.

JOHN DUDLEY.

NOTE.—*Prices quoted in the text are accurate at the time of going to press, but are subject to alteration.*

A.J.S.

Associated Motor Cycles Ltd. of Woolwich produce A.J.S. and Matchless machines, both makes backed by a wealth of racing experience. A.J.S. motor cycles have been to the fore in international competitions for many years, and in 1952 they took the first three places in the Junior Manx Grand Prix, second place in the Senior race, first in the Swiss Grand Prix, and secured 21 world records at Montlhery. There are nine models in the current range, and they are identified this year by a new circular blue badge of polished plastic. The basic engine types are the 350 c.c. single cylinder, the 500 c.c. single cylinder and a 500 c.c. vertical twin.

[*Courtesy: " The Motor Cycle "*

R. M. McINTYRE (348 c.c. A.J.S.) RIDES TO WIN THE 1952 JUNIOR MANX GRAND PRIX

Left : A.J.S. MODEL
16M

Right: A.J.S. MODEL
18S

SPRING TWIN MODEL 20—The 500 c.c. twin with a spring
frame and twinseat is finished, like all A.J.S. machines, in
black with gold lining. It is a powerful touring model with
a high maximum speed and lively acceleration, suitable for
solo or sidecar work. The four-speed gearbox on the A.J.S.
machines was designed for and developed on the famous
7R racing model.

Model	Engine c.c.	B.H.P.	Bore mm.	Stroke mm.	Gearbox
16 M	347 o.h.v.	16/5,600	69	93	4 speed
16 MS	347 o.h.v.	16/5,600	69	93	4 speed
16 MC	347 o.h.v.	16/5,600	69	93	4 speed
16 MCS	347 o.h.v.	16/5,600	69	93	4 speed
18	498 o.h.v.	23/5,400	82.5	93	4 speed
18S	498 o.h.v.	23/5,400	82.5	93	4 speed
18 C	498 o.h.v.	23/5,400	82.5	93	4 speed
18 CS	498 o.h.v.	23/5,400	82.5	93	4 speed
20 "SPRING TWIN"	498 o.h.v.	29/6,800	66	72.8	4 speed

MODEL 16M—The basic machine of the 350 c.c. range has a rigid frame and the usual A.J.S. teledraulic front forks. The 16MS is the spring frame model with a sturdier central stand. A.J.S. rear springing is of the swinging arm pattern, with teledraulic spring units. The tail end of the rear mudguard is detachable on spring frame models for maintenance purposes. The 16MC is the competition "350" with a rigid frame, high ground clearance and polished alloy mudguards. The 16MCS is the springer competition model. (*Concluded on page* 54

Fuel Tank Gallons	Weight lbs.	Wheel Base ins.	Ground Clearance ins.	Carburetter	Total Price £ s. d.
3	343	54	5½	I Amal	172 10 0
3	374	55¼	5½	I Amal	197 8 4
2¼	295	53	6½	I Amal	185 5 7
2¼	320	55¼	6½	I Amal	207 0 0
3	352	54	5½	I Amal	190 7 10
3	385	55¼	5½	I Amal	215 6 1
2¼	297	53	6½	I Amal	203 3 4
2¼	324	55¼	6½	I Amal	224 7 10
4	394	55¼	5½	I Amal	249 16 1

AMBASSADOR EMBASSY

AMBASSADOR

Ambassador motor cycles are built at Ascot, Berkshire, and the 1953 range consists of four lightweight models — all powered by the popular 197 c.c. Villiers two-stroke Mark 6E engine, and all with cradle type frames. A feature of all Ambassador motor cycles is the unscratchable hammered metal petrol tank.

EMBASSY—This model is finished in black enamel with the petrol tank in silver grey. Telescopic front forks carry rubber gaiters this year. As on all models, the exhaust pipe is on the near side and is equipped with a silencer. The main difference between this model and the Popular machine is that the latter has girder type forks instead of the telescopic pattern.

Model			Engine c.c.	B.H.P.	Bore mm.	Stroke mm.	Gearbox
POPULAR	...	...	197 two stroke	8.4/4,000	59	72	3 speed
EMBASSY	...	...	197 two stroke	8.4/4,000	59	72	3 speed
SUPREME	...	...	197 two stroke	8.4/4,000	59	72	3 speed
SIDECAR	...	...	197 two stroke	8.4/4,000	59	72	3 speed

AMBASSADOR SUPREME

SUPREME—The most elaborately equipped of the Ambassador motor cycles, the Supreme has " road flow " spring controlled telescopic front forks with rubber gaiters, and plunger pattern rear suspension. The silencer embodies a fishtail, and the streamlined headlamp brackets are integral with the front forks. On the Supreme and the Embassy the name plate on the petrol tank is in chromium, and the Supreme is finished in grey enamel. The S.S. Supreme—a new model for 1953—is similar, but has a self starter operating from a battery carried in two grey panelled containers astride the rear mudguard.

★　　　★　　　★

THE SIDECAR is marketed only as a combination, together with a specially built lightweight sidecar. It is similar to the Embassy but with girder forks, and is finished in black and grey.

Fuel Tank Gallons	Weight lbs.	Wheel Base ins.	Ground Clearance ins.	Carburetter	Total Price £　s.　d.
2⅛	196	46	5	I Villiers	97 2 3
2⅛	199	46	5	I Villiers	118 16 8
2⅛	213	47	5	I Villiers	134 3 4
2⅛	351	46	5	I Villiers	198 1 2

Above: ARIEL MODEL 4G (Mk. I) SQUARE FOUR

Right: W. S. G. PARSONS, ARIEL TEAM RIDER, IN ACTION

[Courtesy: Donald Page

 Ariel motor cycles, built at Selly Oak, Birmingham, range in size from a big four cylinder machine to twins and singles. In fact, the Ariel company is the only British manufacturer now offering four, twin and single cylinder models. This famous make is as popular with clubmen and sporting enthusiasts as with the motor cyclist who seeks a fast and reliable mount for business and pleasure. There are nine machines in the 1953 range, two of which are new. The newcomers are the 4G Mark I, which is a high performance version of the famous Square Four, and the KHA, a high performance version of the vertical twin KH machine. Other models are the single cylinder Hunters (Models VH, VHA and NH), the competition Hunter, and the side valve single cylinder model VB.

★　　　★　　　★

SQUARE FOUR—Often nicknamed the "Squariel," this fine machine has rapid acceleration and petrol consumption of about 60 miles to the gallon. This year it is finished in Wedgwood blue with white lining and chromium fittings. Twin port exhausts emerge from the engine block on each side, and join into one pipe before the silencer. The 997 c.c. four cylinder engine has a surprisingly flexible performance and is quite happy at low speeds in top gear. The new 4G Mark I is a light alloy version with a two port engine.

★　　　★　　　★

HUNTER TWINS—The twin cylinder Ariels have overhead valve 497 c.c. engines, the new KHA using aluminium alloys to give a higher performance. The KH model is finished in deep claret with gold lining, and the KHA in blue with white lining. All Ariel machines have cradle type frames, and spring frames are an extra.

★　　　★　　　★

HUNTER SINGLES—There are three single cylinder Hunters, two of them 500 c.c. models (VH and VHA) and one with a 350 c.c. engine (NH). The engines have overhead valves, the VHA being a light alloy version of the VH. The VH is finished in deep claret, the VHA in blue, and the NH in black with a red tank. In addition there is the Competition Hunter, with increased ground clearance, an upswept exhaust, and light mudguards—finished in claret—and the side valve 600 c.c. single cylinder (VB), which is finished in black with a blue or green petrol tank.

ARIEL K.H. 500 c.c. HUNTER SINGLE

ARIEL

Model	Engine c.c.	B.H.P.	Bore mm.	Stroke mm.	Gearbox
SQUARE FOUR 4G, Mk. I	997 o.h.v. 4 cyl.	35/5,600	65	75	4 speed
SQUARE FOUR 4G, Mk. II	997 o.h.v. 4 cyl.	40/5,600	65	75	4 speed
HUNTER TWIN KH	498 o.h.v.	26/6,500	63	80	4 speed
HUNTER TWIN KHA	498 o.h.v.	26/6,500	63	80	4 speed
HUNTER SINGLE VH	497 o.h.v.	24.6/6,000	81.8	95	4 speed
HUNTER SINGLE VHA	497 o.h.v.	24.6/6,000	81.8	95	4 speed
HUNTER SINGLE NH	347 o.h.v.	19.4/5,600	72	85	4 speed
MODEL VB... ...	598 s.v.	15.5/4,400	86.4	102	4 speed
COMPETITION HUNTER VCH	497 o.h.v.	26/6,000	81.8	95	4 speed

ARIEL K.H. 500 c.c. HUNTER TWIN

SPECIFICATIONS

Fuel Tank Gallons	Weight lbs.	Wheel Base ins.	Ground Clearance ins.	Carburetter	Total Price* £ s. d.
5	425	56	5½	1 Solex	281 2 3
5	425	56	5½	1 Solex	287 10 0
4	384	56	5½	1 Amal	222 6 8
4	370	56	5½	1 Amal	235 2 3
3½	375	56	5½	1 Amal	194 4 5
3½	360	56	5½	1 Amal	207 0 0
2¾	348	56	5½	1 Amal	172 10 0
3½	362	56	5½	1 Amal	181 8 11
2½	300	54	6½	1 Amal	207 0 0

* Spring frame £20-8-11 extra on all models

B.S.A.

The B.S.A. group, which includes Sunbeam and New Hudson machines (described elsewhere) is responsible for nearly half the annual production of the British motor cycle industry, and has played an important part in the export drive. B.S.A. motor cycles have secured many competition successes. The firm's latest achievement was to win the Maudes Trophy for the most meritorious motor cycling performance of the year by covering 4,958 miles in 24 days on the Continent with three machines taken at random from the production line. This feat included participation in the 1952 International Six Days Trial, in which the B.S.A.'s each won a gold medal and were the only British team to finish with a clean sheet. A comprehensive range of models is offered by the B.S.A. company, varying in size and performance from the popular little Bantam to the big Gold Flash.

Left: B.S.A. GOLDEN FLASH 650c.c. O.H.V MODEL A10

Top right : B.S.A. 250 c.c. O.H.V. MODEL WITH SPRING FRAME

Centre right : B.S.A. GOLD STAR

Bottom right : B.S.A. 500 c.c. S.V. MODEL M21

D GROUP—This group consists of the 125 c.c. two stroke Bantam models with varying specifications. This lightweight is often to be seen on the road finished in pastel green with cream petrol tank panels. It has telescopic front forks with rubber gaiters. One model has a rigid frame, the other two have spring frames with plunger springing. In addition a rigid and a springer competition models are available with upswept exhausts and large section rear tyres. The top speed is about 50 m.p.h., and the petrol consumption between 120 and 140 miles per gallon. Some provincial police forces are using Bantams as patrol machines.

C GROUP—These are the 250 c.c. machines—one with a side valve engine and the other with overhead valves. Each engine type is available in a rigid frame with a three-speed

gearbox, or in a spring frame and with a choice of four- or three-speed gearbox. These models are finished in black or maroon with chromium and maroon petrol tanks

B GROUP—The models in this group are 350 c.c. and 500 c.c. machines, all powered with overhead valve engines. The B31 and the B33 are available with either rigid or spring frames and are the touring versions with the 350 c.c. and the 500 c.c. engines respectively. The B32 and the B34 are the competition machines with specially tuned engines. In addition the Gold Star models, with either the 350 c.c. or the 500 c.c. engine, have spring frames and many detailed modifications to give a higher performance. The B Group machines are finished in maroon, but the Gold Star machines are in black with silver petrol tanks—the B.S.A. emblem in this case being on a gold star.

Model	Engine c.c.	B.H.P.	Bore mm.	Stroke mm.	Gearbox
DI BANTAM ...	123 two stroke	4.5/5,000	52	58	3 speed
DI COMPETITION	123 two stroke	4.5/5,000	52	58	3 speed
C10	249 s.v.	8/5,000	63	80	3 speed
CII	249 o.h.v.	11/5,400	63	80	3 speed
B31	348 o.h.v.	17/5,500	71	88	4 speed
B32 COMP.	348 o.h.v.	17/5,500	71	88	4 speed
B33	499 o.h.v.	23/5,500	85	88	4 speed
B34 COMP.	499 o.h.v.	23/5,500	85	88	4 speed
B32 GOLD STAR ...	348 o.h.v.	—	71	88	4 speed
B34 GOLD STAR ...	499 o.h.v.	—	85	88	4 speed
M20	496 s.v.	13/4,200	82	94	4 speed
M21	591 s.v.	15/4,000	82	112	4 speed
M33	499 o.h.v.	23/5,000	85	88	4 speed
A7 twin	497 o.h.v.	27/5,800	66	72.6	4 speed
A10 GOLDEN FLASH twin	646 o.h.v.	35/5,750	70	84	4 speed
A7 STAR TWIN ...	497 o.h.v.	31/6,000	66	72.6	4 speed

M GROUP—In this group there are three machines, a 500 c.c. with a side valve engine, another with overhead valves, and a 600 c.c. side valve model. All are available with either spring or rigid frames, and are finished in black with maroon and chromium petrol tanks.

A GROUP—The Twin group—containing two basic machines, the 500 c.c. A7 and the 650 c.c. Golden Flash. The A7 is available only with a spring frame, but the A7 Star Twin has high compression pistons, a sports camshaft and the usual " star " badge. The A7 is finished in maroon with a chromium petrol tank, the Star Twin in pale and dark green. The Golden Flash is in a distinctive beige with a chromium panelled petrol tank. The dual seat in lieu of the normal saddle is an extra on all B.S.A. models. The A7 has a maximum speed of 90 m.p.h., the Golden Flash of 100 m.p.h.

Fuel Tank Gallons	Weight lbs.	Wheel Base ins.	Ground Clearance ins.	Carburetter	Total Price £ s. d.
1¾	167	50	4¾	1 Amal	89 8 11
1¾	174	50	7	1 Amal	95 16 8
2⅛	272	52	4½	1 Amal	127 15 7
2½	280	50	4½	1 Amal	131 12 3
3	364	54	5	1 Amal	167 7 10
3	338	54	6¼	1 Amal	191 7 0
3	368	54	5	1 Amal	179 10 7
3	342	54	6¼	1 Amal	203 3 4
3	372	54¾	6¼	1 Amal	245 0 4
3	375	54¾	6¼	1 Amal	255 4 9
3	336	54	5½	1 Amal	168 13 4
3	370	54	5½	1 Amal	172 10 0
3	374	54	5½	1 Amal	178 17 10
3½	400	54¾	4½	1 Amal	220 8 4
4¼	408	54¾	4½	1 Amal	227 8 11
3½	401	54¾	4½	1 Amal	230 0 0

COMMANDER

Most of the motor cycles appearing in this book are made by firms with many years experience of motor cycle manufacture. Here is a machine which only appeared in 1952—made by the General Steel and Iron Company of Hayes, Middlesex as their first venture in the motor cycle industry.

★　　　★　　　★

COMMANDER LIGHTWEIGHT MODEL—A newcomer is always the subject of interest, but this is a truly remarkable machine employing many unusual features, and is quite distinctive in appearance. The chromium-plated grille round the front of the engine, and cowling in other positions, including the partial enclosure of the rear wheel, help to make it an unusually clean machine to ride. The headlamp has a fluted lens which conforms with the futuristic appearance of the machine, and the efficient rear light can be seen through more than 180 degrees. Front springing is by elastic controlled forks and there is swinging arm rear suspension.

Three machines will be available ; the de luxe Autocycle, and the Ultra Lightweight motor cycle (both 98 c.c. Villiers engines), and the Lightweight motor cycle (122 c.c. Villiers). The Ultra Lightweight is finished in maroon and has a road speed of 45 m.p.h. with a petrol consumption of about 160 m.p.g. The Lightweight, in dark blue and cream, has a top speed of 55 m.p.h. and a petrol consumption of some 120 m.p.g. Legshields, windshields, carriers and dual seats are extras.

★　　　★　　　★

Right : THE NEW COMMANDER LIGHTWEIGHT

★　　　★　　　★

Model	Engine c.c.	B.H.P.	Bore mm.	Stroke mm.	Gearbox
DE LUXE AUTOCYCLE	98 two stroke	2.8/4,000	47	57	I speed
ULTRA LIGHTWEIGHT	98 two stroke	2.8/4,000	47	57	2 speed
LIGHTWEIGHT ...	122 two stroke	4.8/4,400	50	62	3 speed

16

Fuel Tank Gallons	Weight lbs.	Wheel Base ins.	Ground Clearance ins.	Carburetter	Total Price £ s. d.
1¼	170	53½	5	1 Villiers	74 19 6
1¼	170	53½	5	1 Villiers	84 19 6
1¼	175	53½	5	1 Villiers	95 16 8

B

DOUGLAS

The Douglas Company of Bristol is the only British motor cycle manufacturer to use a horizontally opposed twin cylinder air cooled engine, which is set transversely in the frame. The Mark V is a popular model among specialist 350 c.c. machines, and, with two higher performance models—the 80 Plus and the 90 Plus—makes up the current Douglas range. This year external oil pipes are a new feature. Douglas machines are used in Finland by the Forestry Commission, and the factory is fulfilling orders from countries as far away as Japan, Morocco and Uruguay.

Left : DOUGLAS MARK V 350 c.c.

Right : P. M. ELVIN RIDES A DOUGLAS IN THE 1952 JUNIOR CLUBMAN'S T.T.

[*Courtesy :* " The Motor Cycle "

MARK V—This has dual chromium-plated exhaust pipes fitted with silencers, and is finished in " Douglas " green. The frame is of the cradle type with torsion bar rear suspension operating through swinging rear forks. The front forks use the radiadraulic system. The front mudguard is designed to follow the movement of the wheel through a light but strong stay assembly. Streamlined detachable tool boxes are carried on each side of the rear mudguards. The petrol tank, which has shaped knee pads, is adjustable for height. The 80 Plus and 90 Plus are similar in appearance, but with lower ground clearance, and engines tuned to give a higher power output.

★　　　★　　　★

Model	Engine c.c.	B.H.P.	Bore mm.	Stroke mm.	Gearbox
MARK V	348 flat twin	18/6,000	60.8	60	4 speed
" 80 " PLUS ...	348 flat twin	25/7,000	60.8	60	4 speed
" 90 " PLUS ...	348 flat twin	27/7,000	60.8	60	4 speed

Fuel Tank	Weight lbs.	Wheel Base ins.	Ground Clearance ins.	Carburetter	Total Price £ s. d.		
3½	340	55	6¼	2 Amals	230	0	0
3½	393	54½	5¼	2 Amals	253	0	0
3½	393	54½	5¼	2 Amals	268	6	8

Left : EXCELSIOR
150 c.c. COURIER
MODEL C2

Right : EXCELSIOR
250 c.c. SPORTS
TALISMAN TWIN

EXCELSIOR

One of the very first firms to manufacture a bicycle commercially in this country (in 1874), the Excelsior Company was also one of the first to market a motor cycle as long ago as 1896. Ever since, their products, distinguished by the trade mark of the young man carrying the "banner with the strange device," have been in the first rank of lightweights all over the world. The firm has raced regularly, the lightweight T.T.'s of 1929 and 1933 being among their many successes. The current Excelsior range consists of four basic models—the Talisman, the Roadmaster, the Courier and the Universal. All have front forks of the Excelsior telescopic pattern with rubber gaiters, and the spring frames have coil spring rear suspension.

Model	Engine c.c.	B.H.P.	Bore mm.	Stroke mm.	Gearbox
U1 UNIVERSAL ...	122 two stroke	4.8/4,400	50	62	3 speed
U2 UNIVERSAL ...	122 two stroke	4.8/4,400	50	62	3 speed
C2 COURIER ...	148 two stroke	6/4,500	55	62	3 speed
R1 ROADMASTER	197 two stroke	8.4/4,000	59	72	3 speed
R2 ROADMASTER	197 two stroke	8.4/4,000	59	72	3 speed
TT1 TALISMAN TWIN	244 two stroke	8.5/4,000	50	62	4 speed
ST1 TALISMAN SPORTS TWIN	244 two stroke	9.7/4,000	50	62	4 speed

TALISMAN TWIN—The vertical twin cylinder Excelsior has a 250 c.c. two stroke engine which gives a top speed of about 60 m.p.h. and a high average speed combined with economical fuel consumption. The Talisman Sports Twin has two carburetters which, with other modifications, produces a higher maximum speed. The Talisman is the only 250 c.c. twin on the market.

★　　★　　★

ROADMASTER (R1 and R2)—This fine lightweight is powered by a 197 c.c. two stroke Villiers engine and has a spring frame. The R2 is fitted with an electric horn and a rectified lighting and battery charging set. Both are finished in maroon with cream tank panels and chromium plating.

★　　★　　★

COURIER—The 150 c.c. machine which was introduced in 1953 has a single cylinder Excelsior engine which combines a high road performance with low running costs. Apart from the smaller power unit, the Courier is similar in appearance to the Roadmaster, and is finished in the same colour scheme. The Universal models have a 122 c.c. Villiers two stroke engine.

Fuel Tank Gallons	Weight lbs.	Wheel Base ins.	Ground Clearance ins.	Carburetter	Total Price £ s. d.
2⅝	182	49½	5¼	1 Villiers	Export only
2⅝	194	49½	5¼	1 Villiers	120 2 3
2⅝	222	49½	5½	1 Amal	120 2 3
2⅝	193	49½	5¼	1 Villiers	124 11 8
2⅝	205	49½	5¼	1 Villiers	130 19 5
2⅝	237	51	5¼	1 Amal	159 14 5
3	242	51	5¾	2 Amals	173 15 7

NOTE: ALSO MAKERS OF THE 98 c.c. AUTOBYK

FRANCIS-BARNETT

The Coventry firm of Francis and Barnett have been well known among motor cyclists for many years as makers of high-quality lightweight machines, which have been particularly successful in trials and scrambles all over the country. In addition to a trials machine and a spring-frame scrambler, each powered by either a 122 c.c. or a 197 c.c. Villiers engine, the firm's current products consist of two basic machines, the Merlin and the Falcon.

Left : FRANCIS-BARNETT MERLIN 57, 122 c.c.

Right: E. W. SMITH RIDES A FRANCIS-BARNETT IN THE 1952 COTSWOLD CUP TRIAL

Courtesy: Ray Biddle]

MERLIN—The Merlin 57 has the 122 c.c. Villiers 10D power unit with a three-speed gearbox and petroil lubrication. It is a spring-frame machine, rear suspension being on the swinging fork principle with a hydraulic damper. The front forks are of the telescopic type with rubber gaiters. The Merlin 52 is the rigid-frame model with a straight instead of an upswept exhaust. The Falcon 58 is the spring-frame machine with the 197 c.c. Villiers 6E engine and the Falcon 55 has the same engine in a rigid frame. All models are finished in black or blue with a gold lined petrol tank.

Model		Engine c.c.	B.H.P.	Bore mm.	Stroke mm.	Gearbox
MERLIN 52	...	122 two stroke	4.8/4,400	50	62	3 speed
MERLIN 57	...	122 two stroke	4.8/4,400	50	62	3 speed
FALCON 55	...	197 two stroke	8.4/4,000	59	72	3 speed
FALCON 58	...	197 two stroke	8.4/4,000	59	72	3 speed

Fuel Tank Gallons	Weight lbs.	Wheel Base ins.	Ground Clearance ins.	Carburetter	Total Price £ s. d.
2¼	181	49	5	1 Villiers	101 11 8
(Merlin 53 as 52 but with battery lighting instead of flywheel magneto £107-19-6)					
2¼	212	49	5	1 Villiers	117 11 2
2¼	199	49	5	1 Villiers	117 11 2
(Falcon 54 as 55 but with flywheel magneto lighting instead of battery £111-3-4)					
2¼	218	49	5	1 Villiers	127 2 10

JAMES

Makers of two-wheeled vehicles since 1880, when Harry James began building penny-farthing bicycles at Birmingham, and of motor cycles since 1902, the James Cycle Company of Birmingham is recognised today as one of the leading manufacturers of lightweight machines. All their 1953 models are powered by Villiers two stroke engines. The James Superlux Autocycle is described elsewhere in this book. The motor cycles are the Comet and the Commodore, with 98 c.c. engines, the Cadet with a 122 c.c. engine, the Captain (197 c.c.), and the Commando (197 c.c.). In addition there are de luxe versions of the Comet, the Cadet and the Captain. All machines are finished in maroon with a gold lined petrol tank.

★　　　★　　　★

COMET—An ideal utility motor cycle, especially suitable for the owner who wishes to ride to work. the Comet is one of the cheapest British machines. There are tubular girder type forks, a two-speed gearbox with handlebar control, a direct lighting system with a headlamp dipper, a top speed of 42 m.p.h. and the remarkable fuel consumption of

Left: THE GENTLER SEX TESTS THE PACES OF A JAMES

Top right: JAMES COMET DE LUXE 98 c.c.

Below centre: JAMES 122 c.c. CADET DE LUXE

Bottom right: JAMES 98 c.c. COMMODORE

168 m.p.g. at 30 to 35 m.p.h. The Comet de Luxe has the 4F Villiers engine with a streamlined crankcase.

★　　　★　　　★

COMMODORE—This is an all-weather version of the Comet, which is specially suitable for ladies and owners who have to ride to work without special motor cycling equipment. A development of the Comet, it has generous engine shields which enclose the top and sides of the engine, but with a cooling opening at the front. Top speed is 42 m.p.h. with a petrol consumption, when cruising, of about 170 m.p.g.

★　　　★　　　★

CADET—This sturdy spring-frame machine has the 122 c.c. engine with a top speed of 50 m.p.h. and a petrol consumption of 135 m.p.g. It is suitable for touring and occasional pillion work. Rear springing is by plunger system, and the front forks are of the hydraulic type with plastic gaiters. The Cadet de Luxe is identical to the Captain de Luxe except for the smaller engine.

★　　　★　　　★

CAPTAIN—The 197 c.c. machine will cruise at over 45 m.p.h. with or without a pillion passenger. Top speed is about 58 m.p.h. and petrol consumption about 117 m.p.g. A rigid all-steel frame is used with telescopic front forks. The Captain de Luxe has a spring frame, battery lighting, electric horn, kerb stand and knee grips and a valanced rear mudguard. The Commando trials model has a rigid frame, high ground clearance and trials pattern handlebars.

Model	Engine c.c.	B.H.P.	Bore mm.	Stroke mm.	Gearbox
J10 COMET	98 two stroke	2.8/4,000	47	57	2 speed
J3 COMET DE LUXE	98 two stroke	2.8/4,000	47	57	2 speed
J4 COMMODORE	98 two stroke	2.8/4,000	47	57	2 speed
J5 CADET	122 two stroke	4.8/4,400	50	62	3 speed
J6 CADET DE LUXE	122 two stroke	4.8/4,400	50	62	3 speed
J7 CAPTAIN ...	197 two stroke	8.4/4,000	59	72	3 speed
J8 CAPTAIN DE LUXE	197 two stroke	8.4/4,000	59	72	3 speed
J9 COMMANDO ...	197 two stroke	8.4/4,000	59	72	3 speed

JAMES CAPTAIN

Fuel Tank Gallons	Weight lbs.	Wheel Base ins.	Ground Clearance ins.	Carburetter	Total Price £ s. d.		
1½	132	46½	6	1 Villiers	70	5	7
2	150	46½	5½	1 Villiers	83	1	1
2	144	46½	6	1 Villiers	83	1	1
2	166	50	5	1 Villiers	89	8	11
2¼	205	49	6	1 Villiers	116	18	4
2¼	185	49	6	1 Villiers	113	1	8
2¼	220	49	6	1 Villiers	127	9	2
2¼	196	49	8½	1 Villiers	134	3	4

 *Matchless machines are built by Associated Motor Cycles Ltd. at Woolwich with A.J.S. motor cycles and, like their stable companions, have a reputation for toughness and reliability in touring and competition work. In 1952 the machine illustrated (facing page) won the Senior Manx Grand Prix, ridden by D. K. Farrant at over 88 m.p.h. The Matchless range, which is exactly parallel to that of A.J.S., consists of three basic machines—the 350 c.c. G3L, the 500 c.c. G80 and the 500 c.c. twin cylinder Super Clubman. All machines have teledraulic front forks, and each basic model is made in a range of rigid and spring frame touring and competition types.*

★   ★   ★

MODEL G3L—The basic 350 c.c. machine has a welded steel petrol tank finished in black enamel and bearing the usual neat winged M emblem. There is an adjustable spring seat saddle, and the machine has a rigid frame. The G3LS is the springer model with teledraulic rear suspension, and the G3LC and G3LCS are the rigid and springer competition machines with light mudguards and competition type exhaust pipes.

★   ★   ★

MODEL G80—The 500 c.c. model—identical to the G3L except for the engine. The G80S is the springer version, and the 500 c.c. Competition machines correspond to the same types in the " 350 " range.

Model			Engine c.c.	B.H.P.	Bore mm.	Stroke mm.	Gearbox
G3L	...	...	347 o.h.v.	16/5,600	69	93	4 speed
G3LS	...	...	347 o.h.v.	16/5,600	69	93	4 speed
G3LC	...	...	347 o.h.v.	16/5,600	69	93	4 speed
G3LCS	...	...	347 o.h.v.	16/5,600	69	93	4 speed
G80	...	...	498 o.h.v.	23/5,400	82.5	93	4 speed
G80S	...	...	498 o.h.v.	23/5,400	82.5	93	4 speed
G80C	...	...	498 o.h.v.	23/5,400	82.5	93	4 speed
G80CS	...	...	498 o.h.v.	23/5,400	82.5	93	4 speed
G9 TWIN	...	...	498 o.h.v.	29/6,800	66	72.8	4 speed

[Courtesy: "The Motor Cycle"

D. K. FARRANT WINS THE 1952 SENIOR MANX GRAND PRIX ON A 498 c.c.
MATCHLESS

MODEL G9 SUPER CLUBMAN—This is the vertical twin
model, which corresponds to the A.J.S. Spring Twin. It
has teledraulic rear springing, and a Dunlopillo twinseat.
The twin exhaust pipes are fitted with megaphones. This
fine machine should be quite easily distinguishable among
the " heavies."

Fuel Tank Gallons	Weight lbs.	Wheel Base ins.	Ground Clearance ins.	Carburetter	Total Price £ s. d.		
3	344	54	5½	I Amal	172	10	0
3	375	55¼	5½	I Amal	197	8	4
2¼	295	53	6¼	I Amal	185	5	7
2¼	320	55¼	6¼	I Amal	207	0	0
3	353	54	5½	I Amal	190	7	10
3	385	55¼	5½	I Amal	215	6	1
2¼	297	53	6¼	I Amal	203	3	4
2¼	324	55¼	6¼	I Amal	224	7	10
3½	394	55¼	5½	I Amal	248	10	6

Above right: MATCHLESS MODEL G3L 350 c.c.
Below right: MATCHLESS MODEL G9,500 c.c. TWIN SUPER CLUBMAN

Above left: MATCHLESS G80 (COMPETITION)
Below left: MATCHLESS MODEL G80S 500 c.c., SPRING FRAME

Whenever international motor cycle racing is discussed the name of Norton is sure to crop up—for this British firm have at one time or another won most of the big events abroad and at home. The Norton score of Tourist Trophy victories is now 28, and this year Nortons hold the Junior, Sidecar, and Manufacturers' Titles in the World's Road Racing Championship. Nortons have utilised their unique racing experience to effect improvements in their production models, which are, today, among our most valuable exports. For 1953 Nortons have replaced the plunger type rear suspension with a new pivot fork system which has been used on their racing machines. Of seven machines for the home market, two have side valves, the remainder overhead valves.

★　　　★　　　★

BIG FOUR—This is an old favourite, being based on a Norton design which was popular 40 years ago. It is still much in demand, particularly as a sidecar machine. The engine, the biggest in the Norton range, is the side valve 596 c.c. with a horsepower of 6.3. The name of the machine dates from the original rating. The Big Four has the usual Norton silver petrol tank with black and red lining. The 16H is built to the same specification, but has a smaller side valve engine.

★　　　★　　　★

MODEL ES2—Another design of long standing with many improvements of recent date, the ES2 is a fast touring machine with the swinging arm spring frame and an overhead valve 490 c.c. engine. The Model 18 is similar, but has a rigid frame.

★　　　★　　　★

DOMINATOR—A fast tourer powered by the 497 c.c. overhead valve vertical twin engine, the Dominator is one of the fastest 500 c.c. production twins in the world. It is now fitted with swinging arm rear wheel suspension and has the usual Norton " Roadholder " telescopic front forks. The Dominator de Luxe has the famous Norton " featherbed " racing frame, similar to that used by the road racing machines with such success.

★　　　★　　　★

500T—This model has a light triangular frame mounting the 490 c.c. vertical twin engine. It is not fitted with the dual seat as a standard fitting, and it is also recognisable by its upswept exhaust.

GEOFFREY DUKE WINS
THE 1952 SENIOR T.T.
ON A NORTON

BIG 4

Model	Engine c.c.	B.H.P.	Bore mm.	Stroke mm.	Gearbox
BIG FOUR	596 s.v.	15.5/4,500	82	113	4 speed
16H	490 s.v.	13.5/4,800	79	100	4 speed
18	490 o.h.v.	25/5,300	79	100	4 speed
ES2	490 o.h.v.	25/5,300	79	100	4 speed
500T	490 o.h.v.	24/5,300	79	100	4 speed
DOMINATOR TWIN	497 o.h.v.	29.5/7,000	66	72.6	4 speed
DOMINATOR DE LUXE TWIN	497 o.h.v.	29.5/7,000	66	72.6	4 speed

NORTON 1952 MODEL
500T 490 c.c.

ES 2

Fuel Tank Gallons	Weight lbs.	Wheel Base ins.	Ground Clearance ins.	Carburetter	Total Price £ s. d.		
3¼	373	54½	5½	1 Amal	190	7	9
3¼	365	54¾	5½	1 Amal	186	11	1
3¼	374	54½	5½	1 Amal	191	13	4
3¼	379	54½	6½	1 Amal	209	11	1
2½	300	53	7½	1 Amal	199	6	8
3¾	413	54½	6½	1 Amal	238	18	11
3½	393	55	5½	1 Amal	265	15	7

 **PANTHER**

Panther motor cycles are made by Phelon and Moore at Cleckheaton in Yorkshire—a district noted for the quality of its engineers—and this Yorkshire firm has been building motor cycles since the beginning of the century. They are particularly well known among motor cyclists for their largest machine, the 600 c.c. Model 100. The 1953 Panther range consists of four machines powered by 250 c.c., 350 c.c. or 600 c.c. engines.

★   ★   ★

MODEL 65—Although it has the smallest engine in the range, this is a man-size motor cycle with a high performance and an attractive appearance. It has telescopic front forks and a rigid frame, but swinging arm rear suspension is also available. The model is finished in blue with cream petrol tank panels lined with gold, and the Panther name plate in gold and blue.

★   ★   ★

THE STROUD MARK III—A sports model with a special alloy engine and an upswept exhaust system for competition work —is available with either the 250 c.c. or the 350 c.c. engine. The mudguards are of polished aluminium, but the finish is otherwise identical to that of the Model 65.

★   ★   ★

MODEL 75—A fine 350 c.c. solo model, the " 75 " is fitted with swinging arm rear suspension of a type developed over a number of years by this firm. It is also available with the rigid frame.

★   ★   ★

MODEL 100—This powerful dual purpose machine is ideal for solo or sidecar work. Phelon and Moore marketed their

Model	Engine c.c.	B.H.P.	Bore mm.	Stroke mm.	Gearbox
65	248 o.h.v.	8.75/5,0C0	60	88	4 speed
STROUD, Mk. III	248 o.h.v.	8.75/5,000	60	88	4 speed
STROUD, Mk. III (alternative)	348 o.h.v.	12/5.000	71	88	4 speed
75	348 o.h.v.	12/5,0C0	71	88	4 speed
100	598 o.h.v.	23/5,C00	87	110	4 speed

[Courtesy: " The Motor Cycle "]
A PANTHER COMBINATION SURMOUNTS A TOUGH SPOT

first 600 c.c. machine early in this century, and a feature of this model for many years—useful for recognition purposes —is the sloping 598 c.c. overhead valve engine, which takes the place of the front down tube of the frame. There are two exhaust pipes in polished aluminium and the model is supplied in grey with a cream petrol tank, panels lined with red and gold. The Panther emblem is in red.

Fuel Tank Gallons	Weight lbs.	Wheel Base ins.	Ground Clearance ins.	Carburetter	Total Price £ s. d.
2⅞	310	54	6	1 Amal	156 10 7
1½	302	54	6	1 Amal	182 1 8
1½	310	54	6	1 Amal	182 1 8
2⅞	315	54	6	1 Amal	171 4 5
3	412	54	6	1 Amal	213 1 5

ROYAL ENFIELD

The Royal Enfield Company of Redditch, Worcestershire, is well-known as a manufacturer of

motor and pedal cycles. *The company, whose slogan is " made like a gun," was founded nearly 60 years ago. The 1953 range consists of eight machines, varying in size from the big Meteor 700 c.c. vertical twin to a little two stroke lightweight. Five of these models are fitted with rear suspension of the swinging arm design, which is becoming increasingly popular. The Royal Enfield motif is carried on the petrol tank of all four stroke models, but is of a slightly different pattern on the two strokes. All machines have telescopic front forks.*

★   ★   ★

R.E. LIGHTWEIGHTS—This, the smallest of the Royal Enfields, has a 125 c.c. two stroke engine and is finished in silver grey. The exhaust pipe is fitted with a chromium silencer and a streamlined expansion chamber. This is a cheap and dependable model which is economical to run and is an ideal machine for the novice. Its top speed is about 50 m.p.h. and petrol consumption between 120 and 150 m.p.g.

★   ★   ★

ENSIGN—This is the second and more powerful two stroke in the range, with a 148 c.c. power unit and a spring frame. It was introduced as a new model for 1953 and is finished in copper beech. Top speed is about 55 m.p.h., with petrol consumption of between 110 and 120 m.p.g.

Model	Engine c.c.	B.H.P.	Bore mm.	Stroke mm.	Gearbox
RE	125 two stroke	4.5/4,500	53.79	55	3 speed
ENSIGN	148 two stroke	5.25/4,500	56	60	3 speed
G	346 o.h.v.	15/5,500	70	90	4 speed
J2	499 o.h.v.	21/4,750	84	90	4 speed
" 350 BULLET " ...	346 o.h.v.	18/5,750	70	90	4 speed
" 500 BULLET " ...	499 o.h.v.	25/5,250	84	90	4 speed
500 TWIN	496 o.h.v.	25/5,750	64	77	4 speed
METEOR 700 TWIN	692 o.h.v.	36/6,000	70	90	4 speed

ROYAL ENFIELD 500 TWIN

MODEL G—This is a 346 c.c. single cylinder model finished in black. Like all the larger Royal Enfields, it has rubber knee grips on the petrol tank. Top speed is in the region of 75 m.p.h. The Model J2 is a 499 c.c. single cylinder touring machine with a top speed of about 85 m.p.h. It, too, is finished in black and there are twin exhaust pipes.

★　　　　★　　　　★

BULLET MODELS—The 346 c.c. Bullet is a single cylinder overhead valve model which has proved to be highly versatile and successful in sporting events. Finished in silver grey and chromium, it has a petrol consumption of between 75 and 80 m.p.g., and a maximum speed of 80 m.p.h. There is also a trials version of this machine. The 500 Bullet is new for 1953. It has a maximum speed of 85 to 90 m.p.h. with a petrol consumption of 70-75 m.p.g.

Fuel Tank Gallons	Weight lbs.	Wheel Base ins.	Ground Clearance ins.	Carburetter	Total Price £ s. d.		
1¾	140	48	5¾	1 Amal	88	3	4
2	155	48	5¾	1 Amal	99	10	2
2¾	370	53½	5¼	1 Amal	166	2	3
2¾	395	54½	4¾	1 Amal	185	5	7
3¼	350	54	6¼	1 Amal	191	13	4
3¼	365	54	6¼	1 Amal	214	0	7
3¼	390	54	5½	1 Amal	233	3	11
4	405	54	5½	1 Amal	245	19	5

Above: ROYAL ENFIELD
R.E. LIGHTWEIGHT

Left: ROYAL ENFIELD
METEOR 700

Below: ROYAL ENFIELD
350 BULLET

500 TWIN—The vertical twin, with a 496 c.c. engine, is finished in silver grey. With a top speed of 90 m.p.h. and a weight only 11 lb. greater than the 500 c.c. Bullet, this is indeed a lively performer.

★　　　★　　　★

METEOR 700—This machine, added to the range for 1953, is the largest capacity vertical twin produced in Britain. It is capable of speeds in the 100 m.p.h. region, and at cruising speeds a petrol consumption of 60 m.p.g. can be attained. By reason of its high power output at low engine speeds it is ideal for sidecar use. The Meteor is finished in copper beech and the dual seat is optional.

TRIUMPH

One of the most famous names in the motor cycle industry is that of Triumph. Their products are to be found not only among the touring machines which throng our roads, but prominent in trials and scrambles and in constant service with many police forces—including the Metropolitan Police. The Trumph Engineering Company, whose factory is at Coventry, has been building motor cycles for over 50 years. Five machines are produced at present—four powered with vertical twin engines and the other with a 150 c.c. single. All have the Triumph four speed gearbox with a foot-operated change, and Triumph telescopic front suspension. The Triumph spring-hub rear suspension is available as an extra.

★　　　★　　　★

THUNDERBIRD—The largest of the Triumphs—is finished in dull blue lined with gold. The speedometer and ammeter are mounted in a nacelle which is integrally built with the top of the forks. An expanding choke type of S.U. carburetter, which was specially designed for this model, provides high performance and fuel economy. The parcels rack mounted on top of the petrol tank is a recognition feature of all Triumph machines—except the Terrier and the Trophy.

★　　　★　　　★

TIGER 100—A sports machine with a 500 c.c. twin engine, the Tiger 100 has a fine competition record. A combined saddle and pillion—the twinseat—is a standard fitting. Alloys have been used extensively on this model to ensure lightness, and a racing conversion kit is available at extra cost. The Tiger 100 is finished in silver and black.

Above: TRIUMPH
THUNDERBIRD

Left : TRIUMPH
SPEED TWIN

SPEED TWIN—A machine which has built up a great reputation
for itself as a fast and reliable tourer, the Speed Twin is
finished in amaranth red lined with gold. It is the cheapest
of the Triumph twins. The Trophy is a lightweight model
designed for cross country work like trials and scrambles.

★   ★   ★

TERRIER—Introduced at the 1952 Motor Cycle Show, this high

Model	Engine c.c.	B.H.P.	Bore mm.	Stroke mm.	Gearbox
THUNDERBIRD TWIN	649 o.h.v.	34/6,300	71	82	4 speed
TIGER 100 TWIN ...	498 o.h.v.	32/6,500	63	80	4 speed
SPEED TWIN ...	498 o.h.v.	27/6,300	63	80	4 speed
TROPHY TWIN ...	498 o.h.v.	25/6,000	63	80	4 speed
TERRIER SINGLE...	149.5 o.h.v.	—	57	58.5	4 speed

Above: TRIUMPH
TERRIER

Right: TRIUMPH
TIGER 100

performance lightweight addition to the Triumph range has a 150 c.c. four stroke engine which is capable of carrying rider and pillion passenger at 60 m.p.h. In most respects the Terrier is very much a scaled down version of the bigger Triumphs, using the same type of front forks and four speed gearbox. The Terrier is a particularly suitable machine for the beginner, because the safety aspect has been carefully studied in its design.

Fuel Tank Gallons	Weight lbs.	Wheel Base ins.	Ground Clearance ins.	Carburetter	Total Price £ s. d.
4	370	55	6	S.U.	219 15 7
4	355	55	6	1 Amal	223 12 3
4	365	55	6	1 Amal	203 3 4
2½	295	53	6½	1 Amal	227 8 11
2¾	175	49	5	1 Amal	125 4 6

SUNBEAM

The massive vertical twin Sunbeam machines are among the elite of the motor cycle world. Their appearance gives an impression of power and stability which is not denied by their performance. Sunbeams are built by the B.S.A. group at Birmingham, and have been chosen by police forces in New Zealand, Khartoum and many other organisations needing robust machines for arduous patrol work. For 1953 there are two machines, similar in most respects, but with detailed differences. They are the S7 and the S8.

★　　　★　　　★

S7—The feature of the Sunbeam twin engines is that transmission is by shaft drive. There is an overhead camshaft and car type lubrication. This, together with the rubber mounted engine, and the spring frame, provides a remarkably quiet running machine. The front forks are of the telescopic pattern, and their tapered shape should be noted as a recognition point. Note, too, the ammeter and switch on the offside of the battery box. The S7 has a saddle mounted on a spring cradle which is adjustable for the driver's weight, and large section tyres. It is finished in mist green with a black frame. Maximum speed is about 80 m.p.h.

★　　　★　　　★

S8—This is a lighter version with a three point spring saddle and smaller section tyres. Its lightness gives a considerable gain

Model			Engine c.c.	B.H.P.	Bore mm.	Stroke mm.	Gearbox
S7 TWIN	...	...	487 o.h.c.	25/5,800	70	63.5	4 speed
S8 TWIN	...	...	487 o.h.c.	25/5,800	70	63.5	4 speed

[Courtesy: " Motor Cycling "

A SUNBEAM COMBINATION

in performance with only fractional sacrifice of comfort. The S8 is finished in black lustre or silver grey. Rear suspension on both models is by totally enclosed plunger springs. Mudguards are domed and valanced, and the rear mudguard hinged. The machine is capable of 85 m.p.h. in solo form.

Fuel Tank Gallons	Weight lbs.	Wheel Base ins.	Ground Clearance ins.	Carburetter	Total Price £ s. d.
3½	430	57	4½	I Amal	281 2 3
3½	405	57	5⅛	I Amal	255 II 2

VELOCETTE L.E. LIGHTWEIGHT

VELOCETTE

A British firm with a long history, Velocette Ltd. of Hall Green, Birmingham, has made use of more than 50 years of successful racing experience in the construction of production models of fine quality and performance. It is particularly in the 350 c.c. class of road racing that Velocettes have made their mark, and they have been certified world champions in this class on several occasions. The current range for the home market consists of the L.E. Lightweight and the M.A.C 350 c.c. machine ; a spring frame version of the M.A.C. is for export only.

Model	Engine c.c.	B.H.P.	Bore mm.	Stroke mm.	Gearbox
Mk. II LE TWIN ...	192 s.v.	8/5,000	50	49	3 speed
MAC	349 o.h.v.	14/5,000	68	96	4 speed

THE L.E.—A luxury lightweight touring machine, which was introduced in 1948 and has since been improved, the L.E. is quite distinctive in appearance. It has a horizontally opposed twin cylinder water cooled engine of 192 c.c., with shaft drive. All moving parts except the roadwheels are enclosed, and deep mudguards, leg shields and footboards make it an exceptionally clean machine to ride. Pannier bags are a standard fitting. Petrol consumption is about

VELOCETTE M.A.C.

100 m.p.g. and the maximum speed about 55 m.p.h. There is a hand operated gear change and telescopic front suspension. The L.E. Model is finished in silver grey, black and chromium.

★   ★   ★

THE M.A.C.—For the home market this model has a rigid frame, and is finished in black and chromium with a black and gold petrol tank. There are telescopic front forks, a fat exhaust silencer and fishtail, and a pillion seat. Top speed is about 70 m.p.h.

Fuel Tank Gallons	Weight lbs.	Wheel Base ins.	Ground Clearance ins.	Carburetter	Total Price £ s. d.
1¼	250	51¼	4½	I	173 15 7
2½	320	52¼	5	I Amal	191 0 0

VINCENT   *The Vincent company, makers of high performance racing, sports and touring machines which are exported all over the world, dates from 1928 when the former H.R.D. company was taken over and re-formed by Mr. Philip Vincent. H.R.D. was dropped from the title in 1952. The factory is at Stevenage, Hertfordshire. The current range consists of a single cylinder 500 c.c. machine*

45

VINCENT 998 c.c.
BLACK LIGHTNING

and three vee twin models. All Vincents are of frameless construction and have aluminium alloy cylinder heads, pistons and crankcases.

COMET—This is a 500 c.c. sports model with a maximum speed of 95 m.p.h. and a cruising speed of 60 m.p.h. The dual seat of moulded Dunlopillo is used on all Vincent machines, and the petrol tank is finished in black with gold lining. The mudguards are of polished alloy, but heavy steel valanced mudguards in black can be supplied at extra cost. The front suspension system used on all models retains the girder principle with very long springs in telescopic cases to provide a long soft action. Petrol consumption is about 80 m.p.g. The Grey Flash is the 500 c.c. racing machine.

★　　　★　　　★

RAPIDE—A vee twin 1,000 c.c. touring model, the Rapide has two exhaust pipes joining in the silencer on the off side. Apart from the larger power unit, the Rapide is similar in appearance to the Comet. It has a maximum of 110 m.p.h., and petrol consumption is 55 to 65 m.p.g.

★　　　★　　　★

BLACK SHADOW—This is the sports version of the vee twin with a top speed of 125 m.p.h. and a cruising speed of *(Concluded on page* 53)

Model	Engine c.c.	B.H.P.	Bore m.m.	Stroke m.m.	Gearbox
COMET	499 o.h.v.	28/5,800	84	90	4 speed
RAPIDE TWIN ...	998 o.h.v.	45/5,500	84	90	4 speed
BLACK SHADOW TWIN	998 o.h.v.	55/5,800	84	90	4 speed
BLACK LIGHTNING TWIN	998 o.h.v.	—	84	90	4 speed

Above: VINCENT 998 c.c. RAPIDE

Below : VINCENT 998 c.c. BLACK SHADOW

Fuel Tank Gallons	Weight lbs.	Wheel Base ins.	Ground Clearance ins.	Carburetter	Total Price £ s. d.
3½	390	57¾	6	I Amal	274 14 5
3½	455	57¾	6	2 Amals	347 11 1
3½	458	57¾	6	2 Amals	389 14 5
3½	380	57¾	6½	Racing Amal	504 14 5

PART II—AUTOCYCLES AND THREEWHEELERS

A. C. PETITE

A newcomer to the range of British three-wheelers is the Petite, which will be on the market in 1953, and is made by A.C. Cars Ltd. of Thames Ditton, Surrey—a firm which produced a three-wheeler before the 1914 war. Although selling at a relatively high price, this little car offers an attractive performance, good accommodation and a smooth ride, with independent springing to all three wheels.

The Petite has a single cylinder 346 c.c. Villiers two stroke engine mounted at the rear. The body is of light aluminium panelling, and has two doors and an easily operated roll-type hood. Its weight brings it within the £5 a year road tax category, yet it can carry two adults and their luggage, or one adult and two children. With a petrol consumption of 60 to 70 m.p.g. and a maximum speed in excess of 40 m.p.h., the Petite makes an ideal runabout. Head and side lights are built into the wings, which partly conceal all three wheels. The frontal motif consists of four horizontal bars surmounted by the maker's badge.

Engine: 346 c.c. (2 stroke)	Gearbox: 3 speed	Wheel Base: 72 ins.
B.H.P.: 8.1/3,750	Fuel: 3 gallons	Ground Clearance: 6¼ ins.
Bore: 70 mm.	Weight: 840 lbs.	Total Price: £398 10s. 0d.
Stroke: 90 mm.		

BOND The latest version of the now famous Bond Minicar—the Mark C—incorporates a number of improvements and the result is an economical three-wheeler with adequate elbow room for two, or even three, passengers—and extremely efficient handling. The Mark C has dummy front wings in which are mounted the combined head and side lights, and an oval radiator grille surmounted by the Bond Minicar emblem. The small rear wheels are provided with separate mudguards.

This latest model has a maximum speed of 50 m.p.h., a cruising speed of 40 to 45 m.p.h., and a petrol consumption of 85 to 90 m.p.g. The Villiers 197 c.c. engine is forward mounted and the front suspension is by a hydraulic shock absorber inside a coil spring. At the rear there are independent bonded rubber units.

Ample luggage space is provided behind the rear seats. Foot brakes operate on all wheels, and there is a separate hand brake on the rear wheels. The Minitruck and the Minivan are the commercial versions of the Bond, which is made by Sharps

Commercials of Preston, Lancashire. Minicars have made many long continental tours with outstanding success, which proves that they are not just " for the local shopping."

Engine: 197 c.c. (2 stroke)	Gearbox: 3 speed	Wheel Base: 66 ins.
B.H.P.: 8.4/4,000	Fuel: 2½ gallons	Ground Clearance: 7 ins.
Bore: 59 mm.	Weight: 450 lbs.	Total Price: £355 0s. 0d.
Stroke: 72 mm.		

CORGI

Here is a scooter with a history. The Corgi, now produced in its civilian guise by the Brockhouse Engineering Company of Southport, is the ancestor of the Welbike, which was specially designed and produced during the war to be dropped by parachute and used as a miniature motor cycle by parachute troops in action. It was used in this role on many famous occasions.

The Corgi retains its wartime characteristic of folding into a comparatively small compass— 56 in. long, 19 in. wide and 25 in. high. Powered by a 98 c.c. Spryt two stroke engine with a two speed gearbox, it is easy to handle and excellent weather protection is provided by the front shield and hinging deep rear mudguard. The front forks are sprung, and a parcel carrier is fitted on the low slung petrol tank. There is an electric horn and a raised headlamp. These machines are available in black, bronze, blue or red with gold lining. The Brockhouse company also produces the Indian Brave four stroke motor cycles.

Engine: 98 c.c. (2 stroke)	Gearbox: 2 speed	Wheel Base: 39 ins.
B.H.P.: 2.4/3,750	Fuel Tank: 1¼ gallons	Ground Clearance: 3¾ ins.
Bore: 50 mm.	Weight: 107 lbs.	Total Price: £74 15s. 0d.
Stroke: 50 mm.		

JAMES SUPERLUX

The only James machine in the autocycle class is the Superlux, powered by the 98 c.c. Villiers two stroke engine, which is fitted in the James Comet motor cycle. When it is remembered that the James Company were experimenting with an autocycle as long ago as 1921, it will be realised that the Superlux is the fruit of much experience. It is quiet and efficient in operation, and the makers claim that it can be ridden and maintained by the un-mechanically-minded novice. An adjustable riding position, open frame and low centre of gravity make it a safe machine in traffic or on the open road.

It is a single speed machine and the engine is covered by a cowl with an inspection opening in it. A carrier and deep section mud-guards are fitted. The top speed is about 35 m.p.h., and the Superlux cruises happily at 30 m.p.h., while the petrol consumption of 145 m.p.g. makes it an economical form of transport. In common with other James machines, the Superlux is finished in maroon with gold lining on the petrol tank, which bears the James winged emblem.

Engine: 98 c.c. (2 stroke)	Gearbox: 1 speed	Wheel Base: 49 ins.
B.H.P.: 2.8/4,000	Fuel: 1¼ gallons	Ground Clearance: 6 ins.
Bore: 47 mm.	Weight: 134 lbs.	Total Price: £70 5s. 7d.
Stroke: 57 mm.		

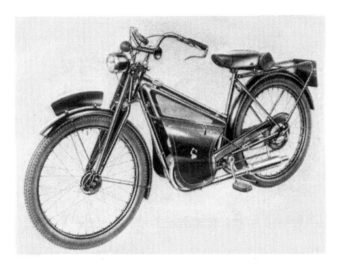

NEW HUDSON

A product of the B.S.A. group of companies, made at Birmingham, the New Hudson autocycle is another example of the economical small powered machine which has many uses in town and country. The engine unit is the new Villiers 98 c.c. Mark 2F with a built-in clutch and flywheel magneto ignition. The frame is of the tubular cradle type, with lightweight motor cycle type spring forks. The rubber mounted petrol tank is slung under the cross-bar and the engine is guarded by a metal shield which descends from each side of the tank. The exhaust system is fitted with a motor cycle type silencer, and an ordinary bulb horn is carried on the handlebars.

The machine is finished in green, the petrol tank having gold lined cream panels, and the engine shields being gold lined with gold transfers of the New Hudson trademark—an arm wielding a sword, emerging from a crown. The New Hudson is simple to start and to ride, cheap to tax and insure, and will cruise happily at 150 miles to the gallon.

Engine: 98 c.c. (2 stroke)	Gearbox: 1 speed	Wheel Base: 50¾ ins.
B.H.P.: 2.8/4,000	Fuel: 1⅝ gallons	Ground Clearance: 5½ins.
Bore: 47 mm.	Weight: 120 lbs.	Total Price: £63 17s. 6d.
Stroke: 57 mm.		

RELIANT

The Reliant Engineering Company (Tamworth) Ltd. have for many years been producing three wheeled commercial vehicles with considerable success, and this year their three-wheeler four-seater coupé is about to go into full-scale production for the private user. A petrol consumption of about 50 m.p.g., combined with a lively performance and plenty of passenger room, is the chief advantage of this economical little machine, known as the Regal.

The power unit is the Reliant side valve 746 c.c. engine which was used in the firm's commercial vehicles. The R.A.C. horsepower rating is 7.5. The coachbuilt body has hard wood framing and metal panels. There are two doors and a hood which can be stowed away in the compartment behind the back seats. This compartment is also designed to accommodate luggage and parcels. Spare wheel, tools and battery are all located beneath the bonnet. The body is finished in gun metal blue.

Engine: 747.5 c.c. (s.v.)	Gearbox: 4 speed	Wheel Base: 84 ins.
B.H.P.: 16/4,000	Fuel: 6 gallons	Ground Clearance: 6 ins.
Bore: 56 mm.	Weight: 890 lbs.	Total Price: £467 7s. 10d.
Stroke: 76 mm.		

VINCENT BLACK SHADOW (*Concluded from page 46*)

100 m.p.h. The engine is almost in the racing category, but the Black Shadow is extraordinarily flexible in traffic and inspires confidence by its road holding and stability at high speed. The Black Lightning is the racing model, and is truly a great performer. It holds American, Australian and South African national solo records and several world and national sidecar records.

VESPA

This scooter is built by Douglas (Sales and Services) Ltd. of Bristol under licence from Piaggio & Co. of Genoa, Italy. It is powered by a lively two stroke 125 c.c. engine concealed under a hinged fairing. The frame is designed to give adequate weather protection. The rear wheel, complete with engine and gearbox unit, is located on a sturdy swinging arm controlled by a helical spring with a separate hydraulic damper. A helical spring is also used at the front. The spare wheel mounted behind the pillion and the windscreen are available at extra cost. The scooter, which is finished in silver green, is capable of over 40 m.p.h., and is remarkably comfortable to ride over the most adverse roads. Commercial sidecar units are also available.

| Engine: 125 c.c.
B.H.P.: 4/4,500
Bore: 56.5 mm.
Stroke: 49.8 mm. | Gearbox: 3 speed
Fuel: 1⅛ gallons
Weight: 170 lbs. | Wheel Base: 44½ ins.
Ground Clearance: 6 ins.
Total Price: £127 15s. 7d. |

A.J.S. (*Concluded from page 5*)

MODEL 18—The basic machine in the 500 c.c. range, the Model 18 is ideal for solo or sidecar work. The engine is of the overhead valve type, similar in detail to the smaller power unit. Other machines in the range are identical to the machines in the 16M range, but with the 500 c.c. engine. All spring frame models have the twin-seat.

Spotting the Numberplate

THE VINCENT
499 c.c. COMET

I—THE LETTERS

THE letters on the number plate tell us by what County or County Borough the motor cycle has been registered. It usually indicates the machine's first registration, but not always ; for sometimes, after a licence has been allowed to lapse for some time, a motor cycle is issued with a new number. Each Registration Authority has one or more two-letter index marks, and they are set out below. Most number plates to-day have three-letter registration marks, but only the last two letters will tell you where the vehicle was registered. For example, the index letters "KLX" indicate that it was registered by the London County Council (see "LX" in the following list).

A	London C.C.	AU	Nottingham C.B.C.
AA	Southampton C.C.	AV	Aberdeenshire C.C.
AB	Worcestershire C.C.	AW	Salop C.C.
AC	Warwick C.C.	AX	Monmouth C.C.
AD	Gloucestershire C.C.	AY	Leicestershire C.C.
AE	Bristol C.B.C.	AZ	Belfast C.B.C.
AF	Cornwall C.C.	**B**	Lancashire C.C.
AG	Ayr C.C.	BA	Salford C.B.C.
AH	Norfolk C.C.	BB	Newcastle-upon-Tyne C.B.C.
AI	Meath C.C.	BC	Leicester C.B.C.
AJ	North Riding of Yorks. C.C.	BD	Northamptonshire C.C.
AK	Bradford C.B.C.	BE	Parts of Lindsey (Lincs.) C.C.
AL	Nottinghamshire C.C.	BG	Birkenhead C.B.C.
AM	Wilts C.C.	BH	Bucks C.C.
AN	West Ham C.B.C.	BI	Monaghan C.C.
AO	Cumberland C.C.	BJ	East Suffolk C.C.
AP	East Sussex C.C.	BK	Portsmouth C.B.C.
AR	Hertford C.C.	BL	Berks C.C.
AS	Nairn C.C.	BM	Bedford C.C.
AT	Kingston-upon-Hull C.B.C.	BN	Bolton C.B.C.

BO	Cardiff C.B.C.
BP	West Sussex C.C.
BR	Sunderland C.B.C.
BS	Orkney C.C.
BT	East Riding of Yorks. C.C.
BU	Oldham C.B.C.
BV	Blackburn C.B.C.
BW	Oxfordshire C.C.
BX	Carmarthen C.C.
BY	Croydon C.B.C.
BZ	Down C.C.

C	West Riding of Yorks. C.C.
CA	Denbigh C.C.
CB	Blackburn C.B.C.
CC	Caernarvon C.C.
CD	Brighton C.B.C.
CE	Cambridge C.C.
CF	West Suffolk C.C.
CG	Southampton C.C.
CH	Derby C.B.C.
CI	Laoighis C.C.
CJ	Hereford C.C.
CK	Preston C.B.C.
CL	Norwich C.B.C.
CM	Birkenhead C.B.C.
CN	Gateshead C.B.C.
CO	Plymouth C.B.C.
CP	Halifax B.C.
CR	Southampton C.B.C.
CS	Ayr C.C.
CT	Parts of Kesteven (Lincs.) C.C.
CU	South Shields C.B.C.
CV	Cornwall C.C.
CW	Burnley C.B.C.
CX	Huddersfield C.B.C.
CY	Swansea C.B.C.
CZ	Belfast C.B.C.

D	Kent C.C.
DA	Wolverhampton C.B.C.
DB	Stockport C.B.C.
DC	Middlesbrough C.B.C.
DD	Gloucestershire C.C.
DE	Pembroke C.C.
DF	Gloucestershire C.C.
DG	Gloucestershire C.C.
DH	Walsall C.B.C.
DI	Roscommon C.C.
DJ	St. Helens C.B.C.
DK	Rochdale C.B.C.
DL	Isle of Wight
DM	Flint C.C.
DN	York C.B.C.
DO	Parts of Holland (Lincs.) C.C.
DP	Reading C.B.C.
DR	Plymouth C.B.C.
DS	Peebles C.C.
DT	Doncaster C.B.C.
DU	Coventry C.B.C.
DV	Devon C.C.

DW	Newport (Mon.) C.B.C.
DX	Ipswich C.B.C.
DY	Hastings C.B.C.
DZ	Antrim C.C.

E	Staffordshire C.C.
EA	West Bromwich C.B.C.
EB	Isle of Ely C.C.
EC	Westmorland C.C.
ED	Warrington C.B.C.
EE	Grimsby C.B.C.
EF	West Hartlepool C.B.C.
EG	Peterborough, Soke of, C.C.
EH	Stoke-on-Trent C.B.C.
EI	Sligo C.C.
EJ	Cardigan C.C.
EK	Wigan C.B.C.
EL	Bournemouth C.B.C.
EM	Bootle C.B.C.
EN	Bury C.B.C.
EO	Barrow-in-Furness C.B.C.
EP	Montgomery C.C.
ER	Cambridge C.C.
ES	Perth C.C.
ET	Rotherham C.B.C.
EU	Breconshire C.C.
EV	Essex C.C.
EW	Huntingdon C.C.
EX	Great Yarmouth C.B.C.
EY	Anglesey C.C.
EZ	Belfast C.B.C.

F	Essex C.C.
FA	Burton-on-Trent C.B.C.
FB	Bath C.B.C.
FC	Oxford C.B.C.
FD	Dudley C.B.C.
FE	Lincoln C.B.C.
FF	Merioneth C.C.
FG	Fife C.C.
FH	Gloucester C.B.C.
FI	N. Riding of Tipperary C.C.
FJ	Exeter C.B.C.
FK	Worcester C.B.C.
FL	Peterborough, Soke of, C.C.
FM	Chester C.B.C.
FN	Canterbury C.B.C.
FO	Radnor C.C.
FP	Rutland C.C.
FR	Blackpool C.B.C.
FS	Edinburgh B.C.
FT	Tynemouth C.B.C.
FU	Parts of Lindsey (Lins.) C.C.
FV	Blackpool C.B.C.
FW	Parts of Lindsey (Lins.) C.C.
FX	Dorset C.C.
FY	Southport B.C.
FZ	Belfast C.B.C.

G	Glasgow B.C.
GA	Glasgow B.C.

GB	Glasgow B.C.		1M	Galway C.C.
GC	London C.C.		1N	Kerry C.C.
GD	Glasgow B.C.		1O	Kildare C.C.
GE	Glasgow B.C.		1P	Kilkenny C.C.
GF	London C.C.		1R	Offaly C.C.
GG	Glasgow B.C.		1T	Leitrim C.C.
GH	London C.C.		1U	Limerick C.C.
GJ	London C.C.		1W	Londonderry C.C.
GK	London C.C.		1X	Longford C.C.
GL	Bath C.B.C.		1Y	Louth C.C.
GM	Motherwell and Wishaw B.C.		1Z	Mayo C.C.
GN	London C.C.			
GO	London C.C.			
GP	London C.C.		**J**	Durham C.C.
GR	Sunderland C.B.C.		JA	Stockport C.B.C.
GS	Perth C.C.		JB	Berks C.C.
GT	London C.C.		JC	Caernarvon C.C.
GU	London C.C.		JD	West Ham C.B.C.
GV	West Suffolk C.C.		JE	Isle of Ely C.C.
GW	London C.C.		JF	Leicester C.C.
GX	London C.C.		JG	Canterbury C.B.C.
GY	London C.C.		JH	Hertford C.C.
GZ	Belfast C.B.C.		JI	Tyrone C.C.
			JJ	London C.C.
			JK	Eastbourne C.B.C.
H	Middlesex C.C.		JL	Parts of Holland (Lins.) C.C.
HA	Smethwick C.B.C.		JM	Westmorland C.C.
HB	Merthyr Tydfil C.B.C.		JN	Southend C.B.C.
HC	Eastbourne C.B.C.		JO	Oxford C.B.C.
HD	Dewsbury C.B.C.		JP	Wigan C.B.C.
HE	Barnsley C.B.C.		JR	Northumberland C.C.
HF	Wallasey C.B.C.		JS	Ross and Cromarty C.C.
HG	Burnley C.B.C.		JT	Dorset C.C.
HH	Carlisle C.B.C.		JU	Leicestershire C.C.
HI	S. Riding of Tipperary C.C.		JV	Grimsby C.B.C.
HJ	Southend-on-Sea C.B.C.		JW	Wolverhampton C.B.C.
HK	Essex C.C.		JX	Halifax C.B.C.
HL	Wakefield C.B.C.		JY	Plymouth C.B.C.
HM	East Ham C.B.C.		JZ	Down C.C.
HN	Darlington B.C.			
HO	Southampton C.C.			
HP	Coventry C.B.C.		**K**	Liverpool C.B.C.
HR	Wilts C.C.		KA	Liverpool C.B.C.
HS	Renfrew C.C.		KB	Liverpool C.B.C.
HT	Bristol C.B.C.		KC	Liverpool C.B.C.
HU	Bristol C.B.C.		KD	Liverpool C.B.C.
HV	East Ham C.B.C.		KE	Kent C.C.
HW	Bristol C.B.C.		KF	Liverpool C.B.C.
HX	Middlesex C.C.		KG	Cardiff C.B.C.
HY	Bristol C.B.C.		KH	Kingston-upon-Hull C.B.C.
HZ	Tyrone C.C.		KI	Waterford C.C.
			KJ	Kent C.C.
			KK	Kent C.C.
IA	Antrim C.C.		KL	Kent C.C.
IB	Armagh C.C.		KM	Kent C.C.
IC	Carlow C.C.		KN	Kent C.C.
ID	Cavan C.C.		KO	Kent C.C.
IE	Clare C.C.		KP	Kent C.C.
IF	Cork C.C.		KR	Kent C.C.
IH	Donegal C.C.		KS	Roxburgh C.C.
IJ	Down C.C.		KT	Kent C.C.
IK	Dublin C.C.		KU	Bradford C.B.C.
IL	Fermanagh C.C.		KV	Coventry C.B.C.

KW	Bradford C.B.C.	ND	Manchester C.B.C.
KX	Bucks C.C.	NE	Manchester C.B.C.
KY	Bradford C.B.C.	NF	Manchester C.B.C.
KZ	Antrim C.C.	NG	Norfolk C.C.
		NH	Northampton C.B.C.
		NI	Wicklow C.C.
L	Glamorgan C.C.	NJ	East Sussex C.C.
LA	London C.C.	NK	Hertford C.C.
LB	London C.C.	NL	Northumberland C.C.
LC	London C.C.	NM	Bedford C.C.
LD	London C.C.	NN	Nottinghamshire C.C.
LE	London C.C.	NO	Essex C.C.
LF	London C.C.	NP	Worcestershire C.C.
LG	Cheshire C.C.	NR	Leicestershire C.C.
LH	London C.C.	NS	Sutherland C.C.
LI	Westmeath C.C.	NT	Salop C.C.
LJ	Bournemouth C.B.C.	NU	Derbyshire C.C.
LK	London C.C.	NV	Northamptonshire C.C.
LL	London C.C.	NW	Leeds C.B.C.
LM	London C.C.	NX	Warwick C.C.
LN	London C.C.	NY	Glamorgan C.C.
LO	London C.C.		
LP	London C.C.		
LR	London C.C.	**O**	Birmingham C.B.C.
LS	Selkirk C.C.	OA	Birmingham C.B.C.
LT	London C.C.	OB	Birmingham C.B.C.
LU	London C.C.	OC	Birmingham C.B.C.
LV	Liverpool C.B.C.	OD	Devon C.C.
LW	London C.C.	OE	Birmingham C.B.C.
LX	London C.C.	OF	Birmingham C.B.C.
LY	London C.C.	OG	Birmingham C.B.C.
LZ	Armagh C.C.	OH	Birmingham C.B.C.
		OI	Belfast C.B.C.
M	Cheshire C.C.	OJ	Birmingham C.B.C.
MA	Cheshire C.C.	OK	Birmingham C.B.C.
MB	Cheshire C.C.	OL	Birmingham C.B.C.
MC	Middlesex C.C.	OM	Birmingham C.B.C.
MD	Middlesex C.C.	ON	Birmingham C.B.C.
ME	Middlesex C.C.	OP	Birmingham C.B.C.
MF	Middlesex C.C.	OR	Southampton C.C.
MG	Middlesex C.C.	OS	Wigtown C.C.
MH	Middlesex C.C.	OT	Southampton C.C.
MI	Wexford C.C.	OU	Southampton C.C.
MJ	Bedford C.C.	OV	Birmingham C.B.C.
MK	Middlesex C.C.	OW	Southampton C.B.C.
ML	Middlesex C.C.	OX	Birmingham C.B.C.
MM	Middlesex C.C.	OY	Croydon C.B.C.
MO	Berks C.C.		
MP	Middlesex C.C.	**P**	Surrey C.C.
MR	Wilts C.C.	PA	Surrey C.C.
MS	Stirling C.C.	PB	Surrey C.C.
MT	Middlesex C.C.	PC	Surrey C.C.
MU	Middlesex C.C.	PD	Surrey C.C.
MV	Middlesex C.C.	PE	Surrey C.C.
MW	Wilts C.C.	PF	Surrey C.C.
MX	Middlesex C.C.	PG	Surrey C.C.
MY	Middlesex C.C.	PH	Surrey C.C.
		PI	Cork C.B.C.
N	Manchester C.B.C.	PJ	Surrey C.C.
NA	Manchester C.B.C.	PK	Surrey C.C.
NB	Manchester C.B.C.	PL	Surrey C.C.
NC	Manchester C.B.C.	PM	East Sussex C.C.

PN	East Sussex C.C.	SN	Dumbarton C.C.
PO	West Sussex C.C.	SO	Moray C.C.
	GPO issued to L.C.C. for	SP	Fife C.C.
	G.P.O.	SR	Angus C.C.
PP	Bucks C.C.	SS	East Lothian C.C.
PR	Dorset C.C.	ST	Iverness C.C.
PS	Zetland C.C.	SU	Kincardine C.C.
PT	Durham C.C.	SV	Kinross C.C.
PU	Essex C.C.	SW	Kirkcudbright C.C.
PV	Ipswich C.B.C.	SX	West Lothian C.C.
PW	Norfolk C.C.	SY	Midlothian C.C.
PX	West Sussex C.C.		
PY	North Riding of Yorks. C.C.		

QA	London C.C.	**T**	Devon C.C.
QB	London C.C.	TA	Devon C.C.
QC	London C.C.	TB	Lancashire C.C.
QD	London C.C.	TC	Lancashire C.C.
QE	London C.C.	TD	Lancashire C.C.
QQ	London C.C.	TE	Lancashire C.C.
QS	London C.C.	TF	Lancashire C.C.
		TG	Glamorgan C.C.
		TH	Carmarthen C.C.
R	Derbyshire C.C.	TI	Limerick C.B.C.
RA	Derbyshire C.C.	TJ	Lancashire C.C.
RB	Derbyshire C.C.	TK	Dorset C.C.
RC	Derby C.B.C.	TL	Parts of Kesteven (Lincs.) C.C.
RD	Reading C.B.C.	TM	Bedford C.C.
RE	Staffordshire C.C.	TN	Newcastle-upon-Tyne C.B.C.
RF	Staffordshire C.C.	TO	Nottingham C.B.C.
RG	Aberdeen B.C.	TP	Portsmouth C.B.C.
RH	Kingston-upon-Hull C.B.C.	TR	Southampton C.B.C.
RI	Dublin C.B.C.	TS	Dundee B.C.
RJ	Salford C.B.C.	TT	Devon C.C.
RK	Croydon C.B.C.	TU	Cheshire C.C.
RL	Cornwall C.C.	TV	Nottingham C.B.C.
RM	Cumberland C.C.	TW	Essex C.C.
RN	Preston C.B.C.	TX	Glamorgan C.C.
RO	Hertford C.C.	TY	Northumberland C.C.
RP	Northamptonshire C.C.		
RR	Nottinghamshire C.C.		
RS	Aberdeen B.C.	**U**	Leeds C.B.C.
RT	East Suffolk C.C.	UA	Leeds C.B.C.
RU	Bournemouth C.B.C.	UB	Leeds C.B.C.
RV	Portsmouth C.B.C.	UC	London C.C.
RW	Coventry C.B.C.	UD	Oxfordshire C.C.
RX	Berks. C.C.	UE	Warwick C.C.
RY	Leicester C.B.C.	UF	Brighton C.B.C.
		UG	Leeds C.B.C.
		UH	Cardiff C.B.C.
S	Edinburgh B.C.	UI	Londonderry C.B.C.
SA	Aberdeen C.C.	UJ	Salop C.C.
SB	Argyle C.C.	UK	Wolverhampton C.B.C.
SC	Edinburgh B.C.	UL	London C.C.
SD	Ayr C.C.	UM	Leeds C.B.C.
SE	Banff C.C.	UN	Denbigh C.C.
SF	Edinburgh B.C.	UO	Devon C.C.
SG	Edinburgh B.C.	UP	Durham C.C.
SH	Berwick C.C.	UR	Hertford C.C.
SJ	Bute C.C.	US	Glasgow B.C.
SK	Caithness C.C.	UT	Leicestershire C.C.
SL	Clackmannan C.C.	UU	London C.C.
SM	Dumfries C.C.	UV	London C.C.
		UW	London C.C.

UX	Salop C.C.
UY	Worcestershire C.C.

V	Lanark C.C.
VA	Lanark C.C.
VB	Croydon C.B.C.
VC	Coventry C.B.C.
VD	Lanark C.C.
VE	Cambridge C.C.
VF	Norfolk C.C.
VG	Norwich C.B.C.
VH	Huddersfield C.B.C.
VJ	Hereford C.C.
VK	Newcastle-upon-Tyne C.B.C.
VL	Lincoln C.B.C.
VM	Manchester C.B.C.
VN	North Riding of Yorks. C.C.
VO	Nottinghamshire C.C.
VP	Birmingham C.B.C.
VR	Manchester C.B.C.
VS	Greenock B.C.
VT	Stoke-on-Trent C.B.C.
VU	Manchester C.B.C.
VV	Northampton C.B.C.
VW	Essex C.C.
VX	Essex C.C.
VY	Yorks C.B.C.

W	Sheffield C.B.C.
WA	Sheffield C.B.C.
WB	Sheffield C.B.C.
WD	Warwick C.C.
WE	Sheffield C.B.C.
WF	E. Riding of Yorks. C.C.
WG	Stirling C.C.
WH	Bolton C.B.C.
WI	Waterford C.B.C.
WJ	Sheffield C.B.C.
WK	Coventry C.B.C.
WL	Oxford C.B.C.
WM	Southport C.B.C.
WN	Swansea C.B.C.
WO	Monmouth C.C.
WP	Worcestershire C.C.
WR	W. Riding of Yorks. C.C.
WS	Edinburgh B.C.
WT	W. Riding of Yorks. C.C.
WU	W. Riding of Yorks. C.C.
WV	Wilts C.C.
WW	W. Riding of Yorks. C.C.
WX	W. Riding of Yorks. C.C.
WY	W. Riding of Yorks. C.C.

X	Northumberland C.C.
XA	London C.C.
XB	London C.C.
XC	London C.C.
XD	London C.C.
XE	London C.C.
XF	London C.C.
XG	Middlesbrough C.B.C.

XH	London C.C.
XI	Belfast C.B.C.
XJ	Manchester C.B.C.
XK	London C.C.
XL	London C.C.
XM	London C.C.
XN	London C.C.
XO	London C.C.
XP	London C.C.
XR	London C.C.
XS	Paisley C.C.
XT	London C.C.
XU	London C.C.
XV	London C.C.
XW	London C.C.
XX	London C.C.
XY	London C.C.

Y	Somerset C.C.
YA	Somerset C.C.
YB	Somerset C.C.
YC	Somerset C.C.
YD	Somerset C.C.
YE	London C.C.
YF	London C.C.
YG	West Riding of Yorks. C.C.
YH	London C.C.
YI	Dublin C.C.
YJ	Dundee B.C.
YK	London C.C.
YL	London C.C.
YM	London C.C.
YN	London C.C.
YO	London C.C.
YP	London C.C.
YR	London C.C.
YS	Glasgow B.C.
YT	London C.C.
YU	London C.C.
YV	London C.C.
YW	London C.C.
YX	London C.C.
YY	London C.C.

Z	Dublin C.C.
ZA	Dublin C.C.
ZB	Cork C.C.
ZC	Dublin C.C.
ZD	Dublin C.C.
ZE	Dublin C.C.
ZF	Cork C.C.
ZH	Dublin C.C.
ZI	Dublin C.C.
	Dublin C.C.
ZZ	The Council of any County which adjoins N. Ireland The Royal Irish Automobile Club, Dublin The Automobile Association, Dublin
BZ	British Zone, Germany

60

Spotting the Number-plate

**II—THE
NUMBER
GAME**

HERE is a game which you can play whenever you see a
motor vehicle. The object is to spot registration numbers
in numerical order from 1-999. Challenge a friend to a race,
and remember that neither of you can claim to have begun until
you have spotted a number plate with the number 1. Then go on
to 2 and 3, and so on to 999. You can use the pages which follow
to keep a record of your progress.

1	17	33	49	65
2	18	34	50	66
3	19	35	51	67
4	20	36	52	68
5	21	37	53	69
6	22	38	54	70
7	23	39	55	71
8	24	40	56	72
9	25	41	57	73
10	26	42	58	74
11	27	43	59	75
12	28	44	60	76
13	29	45	61	77
14	30	46	62	78
15	31	47	63	79
16	32	48	64	80

81	129	177	225	273
82	130	178	226	274
83	131	179	227	275
84	132	180	228	276
85	133	181	229	277
86	134	182	230	278
87	135	183	231	279
88	136	184	232	280
89	137	185	233	281
90	138	186	234	282
91	139	187	235	283
92	140	188	236	284
93	141	189	237	285
94	142	190	238	286
95	143	191	239	287
96	144	192	240	288
97	145	193	241	289
98	146	194	242	290
99	147	195	243	291
100	148	196	244	292
101	149	197	245	293
102	150	198	246	294
103.	151	199	247	295
104	152	200	248	296
105	153	201	249	297
106	154	202	250	298
107	155	203	251	299
108	156	204	252	300
109	157	205	253	301
110	158	206	254	302
111	159	207	255	303
112	160	208	256	304
113	161	209	257	305
114	162	210	258	306
115	163	211	259	307
116	164	212	260	308
117	165	213	261	309
118	166	214	262	310
119	167	215	263	311
120	168	216	264	312
121	169	217	265	313
122	170	218	266	314
123	171	219	267	315
124	172	220	268	316
125	173	221	269	317
126	174	222	270	318
127	175	223	271	319
128	176	224	272	320

321	369	417	465	513
322	370	418	466	514
323	371	419	467	515
324	372	420	468	516
325	373	421	469	517
326	374	422	470	518
327	375	423	471	519
328	376	424	472	520
329	377	425	473	521
330	378	426	474	522
331	379	427	475	523
332	380	428	476	524
333	381	429	477	525
334	382	430	478	526
335	383	431	479	527
336	384	432	480	528
337	385	433	481	529
338	386	434	482	530
339	387	435	483	531
340	388	436	484	532
341	389	437	485	533
342	390	438	486	534
343	391	439	487	535
344	392	440	488	536
345	393	441	489	537
346	394	442	490	538
347	395	443	491	539
348	396	444	492	540
349	397	445	493	541
350	398	446	494	542
351	399	447	495	543
352	400	448	496	544
353	401	449	497	545
354	402	450	498	546
355	403	451	499	547
356	404	452	500	548
357	405	453	501	549
358	406	454	502	550
359	407	455	503	551
360	408	456	504	552
361	409	457	505	553
362	410	458	506	554
363	411	459	507	555
364	412	460	508	556
365	413	461	509	557
366	414	462	510	558
367	415	463	511	559
368	416	464	512	560

561	609	657	705	753
562	610	658	706	754
563	611	659	707	755
564	612	660	708	756
565	613	661	709	757
566	614	662	710	758
567	615	663	711	759
568	616	664	712	760
569	617	665	713	761
570	618	666	714	762
571	619	667	715	763
572	620	668	716	764
573	621	669	717	765
574	622	670	718	766
575	623	671	719	767
576	624	672	720	768
577	625	673	721	769
578	626	674	722	770
579	627	675	723	771
580	628	676	724	772
581	629	677	725	773
582	630	678	726	774
583	631	679	727	775
584	632	680	728	776
585	633	681	729	777
586	634	682	730	778
587	635	683	731	779
588	636	684	732	780
589	637	685	733	781
590	638	686	734	782
591	639	687	735	783
592	640	688	736	784
593	641	689	737	785
594	642	690	738	786
595	643	691	739	787
596	644	692	740	788
597	645	693	741	789
598	646	694	742	790
599	647	695	743	791
600	648	696	744	792
601	649	697	745	793
602	650	698	746	794
603	651	699	747	795
604	652	700	748	796
605	653	701	749	797
606	654	702	750	798
607	655	703	751	799
608	656	704	752	800